www.finishinglinepress.com

RUIN PORN

poems by

Terry Wolverton

Finishing Line Press
Georgetown, Kentucky

RUIN
PORN

ACKNOWLEDGMENTS

"Brewed" and "Suspended" were previously published in *Adrienne,*
    Issue #4. 2014.
"Green Fade: Let It Rest" was previously published in *Petrichor Review,*
    issue 8. http://www.petrichorreview.com/issue-8/terry-wolverton/
"Hopscotch Highway" was previously published in *Wide Awake: Poets of
    Los Angeles and Beyond,* edited by Suzanne Lummis, Henry Morro
    and Liz Camfiord. Pacific Coast Poetry Series, Beyond Baroque,
    Venice, California. 2015.
"Imaginary City" and "Origami Portrait" were previously published by
    YAY LA Magazine, 2015.
"In Bed She Invents the Next Millennium" was previously published in
    Whale Road Review, Issue 2, Spring 2016.
"Region/Ambiance" was previously published in *Lummox 2,* edited by
    RD Armstrong, San Pedro, CA. 2013
"Sometimes I Wake Up in September" was previously published in *The
    Mas Tequila Review, 2014.*
"Work" was previously published in "Curator's Essay" by Ariadni A.
    Liokatis, *Drawn to Language,* exhibition catalogue, USC Fisher
    Museum of Art. Los Angeles, CA.

Publisher: Leah Maines

Editor: Christen Kincaid

Cover Art: Yvonne M. Estrada

Author Photo: Yvonne M. Estrada

Cover Design: Elizabeth Maines McCleavy

Printed in the USA on acid-free paper.
Order online: www.finishinglinepress.com
            also available on amazon.com

Author inquiries and mail orders:
Finishing Line Press
P. O. Box 1626
Georgetown, Kentucky 40324
U. S. A.

Table of Contents

Woman in a Skirt of Weather

Roof of the World Torn Away

I'm Re-thinking My Halo

For Yvonne
Siempre

Ruin Porn

I cannot turn away, my eyes
themselves ruins of memory,
lifetimes of nights thrusting
down ferocious boulevards,
now returned to prairie.

Today devours yesterday—
how long since I breathed this blighted air?
Map of recollection faded,
translucent as frozen petals
or dry, inhospitable skin.

My old ghost crouches in collapsed
ballrooms and diners, compiles a
portfolio of years—all gone.
Blown away churches and schools, roofs
caved in, windows cracked and blackened.

I remember shouting, "Power
to the People," an orchid in
my mouth. But flowers couldn't wait;
people left, or died. I left too.
And what streets remain are silent.

I cannot pretend it will be
as it once was. And what was it
anyway? A city? A jail?
A fist? Only shadows remain
and still they pucker on my skin.

Time's Canopy

Time's Canopy

Afternoon
The old cat re-appears at the screen door

3 p.m.
Relax in green shade with an Eskimo pie

Sometimes
Hiding in a bed of grass and leaves

6 p.m.
Orange sun begins to fall into the neglected street

Hours
My grandmother's open hands at the end of her life

Thursday
Sounds of bells outside the window—I hold my breath

Evening
Gratitude for its cool, lavender light

Midnight
Exuberant music of the freeway

Days
A birthday, a party dress, a glass of ginger ale

Summer
Hems of the trees promise a deeper gold

Years
The body a wooden puppet, trying to embrace air before disappearing

Born

You show up to this planet naked, drunk
on gravity. Smile into blue water,
but it bubbles up through your fingertips,
floods your reflection, skin streaming with light,
shoulders melting into lake. This transforms
history, signaling back to mother
and grandparents: no more this origin.

Compass thrown out, the map in flames, turn in
the direction of another garden.
Make a bonfire of language; even
your heart cannot contain the peonies
that emanate from your fully human
lips. Some listen, but do not understand
the evidence you've catalogued: the fact

of your arms, saliva soft in your mouth,
its collection laden with DNA.
Not poor, then, not sick, not strange or crazy,
let sunset embrace this hard land, mother
from whom you came. Trace its blaze back through the
eyes, lit mirrors of deep time. Move into
flowing lake, channel your own happiness.

City Life

Ed the Hype dies from the sting of vision;
he will not mourn the passing of autumn

Crows tell jokes to naked gods who gather
on the corner in the green morning rain

In the parking lot of the liquor store,
matron plays chess with an exhausted thief

All afternoon, two Chihuahuas, little
rats, lick the tears of a wino in the park

The pallbearer's face is sealed; he catches
the hummingbird rising to the new moon.

Bare-limbed girls eat cake like kittens, clicking
heels against moments of the night sidewalk

After work, the workers dress like ladies
for the bonfires on Skid Row at midnight.

Prayers of the lonely go unnoticed;
Star People lift up the sky, flood our eyes.

Scrapes of the world do not erase me. I
find my sunglasses, snatch an hour of song.

Penetrate

Middle of one indigo night
air-to-ground spectacle
on the blasted TV.
          I was naked and overripe.
          She watched from inside her skin.

Everyone fears the burning dark
so they stuff their cheeks
with cartoon colors.
          I was painted green and laughing.
          She carried her morning song.

Haunted with pure spectrum,
kids slump outside laundromats
scorched in pink light.
          I was a cream pie, a chandelier.
          She annealed the bloody past.

What the sun wants: no sunglasses
no sunscreen; let me radiate
through the bleached stupor.
          I was waiting with outstretched chakras.
          She created the rising world.

Elemental Changes

Play the sky radio, its blue soul.
Sip a breath of night; take in its naked mood.
Merge with shadow, fall for darkness.
Remain dangerous.

Notice the pretty walls, aching and damp.
Leave the claustrophobic nest.
Release the ruin of identity.
Shed the clock's chaotic teeth.

Open to crumbling, grow raw and true.
Let the red skin combust.
Pick a new name and tongue its music.
Find the eyes and look often.

Push wings on fire to a hidden landscape.
Do not pause.
Swear to become the catalyst.
Always keep a button of light.

Some Times

I awaken in the clock factory;
tired clerks sell the reddened light of morning.
These exchanges leave my days greasy and slow,
stir gray pale cravings in my belly.
I cannot digest backyard birdsong,
alongside handguns' popping rhythms.

I've trafficked sunrise, worn money like dirt.
I've practiced the karma of robotic
shopping, but while time can be spent cheap,
in the end it will always grind and congeal.
No transaction can dispel the hunger
for beginning again in indigo.

First watch never ends; each daylight lies.
The useless lump of sun burns in my hair.

Songs of Other Worlds

The gatekeeper is useless
asleep at the yellow barrier
carefully guarding the fog

Cats follow a private moon,
its particular gleam on the gutters,
paws moving slowly past time.

A few tough novelists shatter
the whalebone corsets of the mind
to breathe in the trembling air

Lovers spill, all hands,
fat with sunshine and surprise,
into muted streets at 3 a.m.

Thieves unravel cloud strands
in the parched city, slip between
body and imagination

The executioner acts in shadow
while the torn throat empties;
no one can escape this fate

A cabdriver eyes shuttered windows,
music of Paris blossoms on her lips;
she drives fast as the light dims

Behind the towers, a guard
blinks into the quiet dark,
mouths the perfunctory password

Godot waits through the blue night;
after promise collapses,
the fabric of the world is thin.

Margin

Lorene thinks of profits as she carries
the daily special to people who
know no satisfaction. Honey, ham and
mustard—nowhere near sufficient to
rid oneself of emptiness. Lorene knows
about empty; she's got a big red purse
in need of dollars, a secondhand car,
an ugly zebra print costume she has
to wear. Can't seem to unload anything—
not wild longing, not her carbon-dated
nostalgia that lives in the jungle
of mean time. She craves an awakening—
routine trashed, cartoon mask cut away—
no more the old numbers, the sorry cost.

Work

Woman on her knees before the big clock.
Morning is no peach pie, no lemon sun.
Light the new day with violet lanterns,
she begs another sky, its coral roof.

Same story, the room always waiting; hot,
its breezes sour, chemical. Day begins
before the candle melts. Even the dog
on the grounds remembers his zone of rope.

The schedule is turning in her brain,
minutes hanging from dry, tired trees, doubting
theories of twilight. Is she a person
or an explosion in the factory?

The wrong moon colors this night; all the birds
in the green world cannot release her earth song.
Time's sad machine still starts and stops. Dinner
in the shade of the flame lit universe.

Region/Ambiance

Only a rock
in the sea of
well-worn universe,
a bubble travelling
the broken sky,
salt patterns
on the foam of sleep

The teeth of money
and luminous time,
flu water
and river foam,
my unread face
only a copy
of the dark stars

A dream of trees
beneath blue black night,
the bright lie
of unlimited shine,
light leaving
our tiny corner
messy, heaving and red

Tomorrow This Day Will Forget You

Songs of sirens vanish
under moonless shell of night
still the day holds you soaked
in its terrible prayer

Fire makes a game of light
pours like milk through windows,
in the room of the world
hours balloon, then crumble

Helicopters and trucks
on steroids, moans heard even
in dreams, reduce the senses
to noise sweat breath

Kids on the sidewalk, eyes
ground to powder, recipe
of black ash and tears, almost
birdlike in the bowl of your fist

The vipers are puffy
but punishing, gray limbs
twisted, ready to slam
hell into your palate

Pillow swollen with nightmares
you are awake at midnight;
come here to my pretty house,
turn poison to medicine.

Green Fade: Let It Rest

This last summer day. Already we turn
toward darkness, sun collapsing into

ocean's pale skirts. Blood of blueberries
only a memory staining a white dish.

All is aftermath. Now the trees' lacy
crowns eroding to fire. Furling petals

spiral like light in an afternoon breeze.
Our bodies' rhythms rub against the hours.

It's time to study surrender, learn not
to go to war with each leaking moment.

Imagine dancing like queens in winter's
temples, nodding to children in the street.

This morning will not sit with our sadness;
the world is not broken, but born anew.

I Make My Ornery Confession

Red Sweater

Winter cannot remake this ruined
neighborhood, singed by yellow music
of intemperate flame. Houses of
a dying century breathe ash into
the night's silence; stone stairs lead nowhere
before falling toward rutted asphalt.
The dark body curls in on itself.
Branches drink the glass gray air; fields rise.

Once I was a daughter of these bricks;
my hair the color of its fires, limbs
like matchsticks alight. Its graffiti
wears my vacant skin. I stand in the
remains and swallow the dark moods of
water falling, unrelieved, from sky.

Guilt

When I make my ornery confession,
circuitry vibrates with the orange pulse
of my crimes. Density of a half-blown
universe succumbs to swirl; cracks in its
surface reveal the bare, solitary
planet beneath us, a sad strip club in
Candy Land. Hale-Bopp screams through but we don't
look; we plead true innocence and still drink
the last of the Kool-Aid. I am guilty
of an attitude problem, painting my
secrets blacker than yours, sleeping when the
heart train zips by, face catching that red light.
Once my trance dissolves I will taste wonder,
more moon than molecules, at last reformed.

Sometimes I Wake Up in September

Birthdays are pale, unappealing things;
I feel naked to be recognized that way.
I would rather walk down to the river,
my eyesight more conscious there.

At the party I am a dead eggplant—
my mouth keeps exploding with stupid,
I do not recognize a soul
and my fingertips ruin the cake.

So it's summer and the faces keep changing
into flowers and light. You all look like angels,
but hey, why are we in this dark hotel?
I pour evening over my naked appetite.

My mother claims I will understand
when I am older, but time conceals
its face under luxurious orange cloth,
will not explain its vision of tomorrow.

Yesterday is a mattress, tomorrow
a glowing boat. The fruit of days
claims the body; we barely hear
the brighter music of passing seasons.

She Buries Her Passport

On a moonless, metal night,
she buries her passport
under the orange trees;
scent of their blossoms
makes her shadow swoon.

She doesn't believe
in borders, wants to
shuck the gridded earth,
its territory mapped,
marked and measured, claimed,

her body held in a
bubble suit that squeezes
the breath in her rib cage.
She'd rather travel as
a collection of light,

escape gravity
and roots. She'd rather
be a spiral of heat
in the arms of the sky,
so she carries the moon

in her palms, drives deep
into dirt, stretches the edge
of latitude, digs
an uncharted garden
to hold where she's been.

Climate Change

My former mentor, teachers, therapist come
to me one night, spread cold flame around my soul.
We drink up all the Kool-Aid, then we shine red.

This hotel in the desert feels like marble.
White sun settles around us, an aching cloud,
another mocking world, a weather all its own.

Lately people hold discordant music, breathe
the fog of discontent. Keep company with
bitter angels who bother each dream-fired night.

I taste summer in my throat. I take the stairs.
This transforms into speed, somehow I'm flying.
Or only swaying faster, perched in gray air.

I want years to be filled with speed, bright yellow;
you want to hurry past the dark steps of earth.
We jump easily together, wrapped in smoke.

So many angels have broken into my
sour reason. Their stone wings make no sensation
but my bones believe the color, warm deep life.

Passage

After graduation, will I be just
as lost, dizzy from paranoia,
gazing at unmatched shoes on the floor
of this spinning universe?

Once the worn chords of "Pomp
and Circumstance" are struck,
will I find a phase of morning or
just another cabinet of surrender?

Crows will guide me on a parallel
path—romance and weeping,
blouses strangling their hangars
in a Pavlovian closet of night.

How can we graduate? Just re-arrange
the dresses, marry or fall, laugh
or disagree. There is no rite of turning
utterly into someone else.

Perhaps I will always be floating,
no compass or clue, each moment
discarding everything I once
was sure I would be.

Some Small Change

The faithful hawks seemed to patrol the road
in case a car should run off, wheels spinning
into cedar pine, a life stalled, lug nuts
jammed and you can't fix it. They were looking
to snag dinner, their wings shadows in the sky.

I remember you in a blue suit, big
bank account, diet of coffee and cheese,
strumming a ukulele to woo that
moon, a little wafer handmade of paste—
all you promised in that sheltering song.

Me, I'm just a factotum for the dead.
I rise and kneel, mate with power, spend their
status. My horoscope did not predict
a journey to this kill where I wait for
what's next, the twin hawks circling above.

Hopscotch Highway

I should have known better than to wear
the ball gown, the one with a tight waist.
I sweat orange circles into that red
taffeta; my chignon combusted
in the blue wind. I stuck out my thumb
and the sky sneered. Overhead, the crows
were sympathetic, but we all knew
no one luminous was going to pass
this way, not before the gold storm rose.

That moon, she couldn't do a damn thing
for me. I had a rocket in my
belly; I wanted to savor her
from afar. How will I know my heart's
broken? If we come here with just so
many breaths, maybe we come with just
so many tears. Maybe I've dried up,
a lake that's disappeared, residue
of fish bones glinting under the sand.

I Can Recognize Anarchy When I See It

Blown Open

I can recognize anarchy when I see it—
you planting small, warm buttons in the violet earth.

I wanted your fingers to unlatch my spine.
Everything detonating in my wary brain.
Landmines going off in the blood garden.
Wherever I thought I was, revealed to be another world.

If that seems terrible, it was, but I was no victim.
I was a buried planet exposed to pearled light.
I was a river of fire. A star dismantled
in a recent galaxy. Photo of an aching sky.

Before this my face held tight to its metal casing,
jaws packed with wars of remembering,
fiery cities of nothing known or chosen.
Before this, I fished seeds from a blackened shore.

Now my hand curls around this velvet bomb.
You laugh, embrace the innocence you've sown.

Wherever You Are

Sometimes I feel I am performing for
your eyes as I move about the city,
waking on a train, crossing the alley,
surrounded by conversations of others
but wrapped in your song. I carry a blue
scrap of night in my mouth, like a hard seed
about to blossom in its morning bed,
its scent floating on my skin. I watch for
your face in a window, look for that light
beaming at me in the language of a
lost world. You're not there, but I imagine
you on the corner when I turn, clothed in
the skirt of sun you gave me, sky singing
too, soaking me in great-hearted laughter.

Green Honey

If I owned a glass spaceship
I could see all the sad flowers
of the spinning universe.
I would not suffer this world
as a jail or hospital,
nothing but walls of data
to escape. Sickness would leave
my mind, its factoids dispersed
into substance-less vapor.
My eyes would wake to gardens
of milk blue clouds, ice crystals
dissolving like my heartbeats.
I'd visit your atmosphere
to borrow a cup of rain.

The Coat of You

Which is more lasting—sand or scars?
Snow crystals against night sky
or rising on a road of fire?

We could never have known meadows
of bumblebees would not be
permanent, would be replaced by

helicopters illuminating
the startled bones of the city
like rugged moons. Is it harder

to erase touch or to remain
un-etched by those fingerprints?
I can curl myself into the coat

of you, the music of your breath,
but even now shadows fade, just
beyond the surface of the skin.

Gathers

The matron waits alone in her dark chamber
Outside the window morning explodes in her eyes

The girl is a small pearl dropped in a sidewalk puddle
All the world's subterfuge wrapped in her heart

People pour their muted song into the still ocean
It trickles as rain, then becomes ice

Your body is capable of feeling the blue depths
But you lie on your stone mattress in a lightless house

The yellow dress of my breath holds me, grows heavy
I scarcely hear the subtle emptying of mind

Now your mission is one of leaving
Glass to your lips, you slip away into rain

God tricks me with tiny strokes of green
I come to his music, happy to be fooled.

Imaginary City

What remains of the imaginary
city I am from? Have you forgotten
its crescent architecture, its industrial
rain? The Saturday night fandangos through
fitful traffic? Have you swept away all
the errant vows broken like teacups in
an empty basement, music of afternoon leaves?

I suppose it was hard enough to dream
the colorless moon floating heavy above
above its dusty river. We gathered
at water's edge to drink in languorous
clouds, passing orange in the syrupy sky,
to lick softly the last hope from the plate
of asking and contemplation.

When did the itchy allure of meaning
fall into the detritus of long years?
Do you remember I fluttered my frayed
finery, threads hung with favorite toys
like tiny charms, a dress of breeze and light?
Flipped my green hat? We were spoons whispering
by the stove, under a table of sky.

Brewed

we were like stuck puppets
under starry violet
fallen into a pageant of dust
our sleep leaking dreams
all over that sweaty morning

my umbrella open to the rain
a whirlygig spinning
up into shiny trees
but I could not follow
could not climb to green

you relied on the spiders
their webs like earrings
floating around your head
you stopped carrying keys
instead circled your boat on the pond

>   the king wants coronation
>   the lions are singing to the night
>   birds hiding in the library
>   even the cowboys jumping off
>   the high, clear trampoline

in a room beside the alley
under a sky like old tin
smell of coffee, bellies filled with poems
we were pretty, we were tough
shouldn't it have been enough

Jars of Always

Around the auric fields of angels, threads
of frayed, pale light may evidence wounds from
interventions in matters of the world.

Across table, you harbor a shaman's
presence. My eyes on bottom of the dish
your tongue has stirred as if it were my skin.

Between the dirt of the world and moon's light
our fingers try but cannot quite hold on
to any essence that is not finite.

From head to hands, I'm a bad example,
always rolling, never listening, wrong
dog just waiting for divine escapades.

Until sounds of compassion coat my mouth
with shooting stars, I remain caught in my
pet worries, always terrible and new.

Through trouble we find mercy; through mistake
we apprehend. I can generate plans,
rules, but teeth consume time's white hot slurry.

Before you leave, I will look for patterns
in the gems. They will tell me all I could
have done differently to treasure you.

Origami Portrait

When I was a witch
I buried my dreams between the church and midnight.
You learned the poem of me by accident
watching my anatomy.

When I was a man-eater
you placed apples and tomatoes on my pillow,
a small bomb in a pin cushion.
I overlooked our silences.

When I was the fox
you were scared to follow me to the arboretum
Forest of noises set you running;
the last trees listened.

When I was Betty
you dared me to go into the city alone.
I loved the traffic and the parking lots,
the snow days sparking.

Always I was becoming and unbecoming.
A reflection on the water.
A problem to be solved.
A modern curse.

When I was an Eskimo
I found miracles mirrored in the ice and stars.
We were a couple of morning spirits
melting cold, bright towers.

When I was a totem
I saw the wild-eyed world as my fortune cookie.
You looked like murder on a someday night.
We never ended.

Woman in a Skirt of Weather

In Bed She Invents the Next Millennium

She's the one who scrawled graffiti
on the walls of church, imagined
God's tattoos dripped green in the aisle—
stars and fishes rising across time.

Pastor's laughter echoed in her hair,
heavy with the scent of gravy.
She was no angel. She is his
nightmare, an itch in his bloodstream.

She will not climb Heaven's ladder
to the stained sky. She escapes with
the water snake, still carrying
her crayon bouquet. She combusts

on the hot road to someplace else,
distant city where she skids like
a boat in mercury. Her face
a smashed moon in the purple hour.

What is a girl's power? To veer
from the clock's maniacal grin,
bust out of the round house, follow
the blood drops to the other side?

A window, her eye. A rope, her
dress. Platters, a ring—once her home.
She samples sounds of metal on
sidewalk, before Coyote sleeps.

Suspended

It's a cold day for the karma parade.
Everyone holds umbrellas against
the rain but the river is on fire again
and no one can promise it won't explode.
Still the President is on a giraffe
and people think, "What's that guy doing?"
so we are distracted in our burning
world. I'm up on a ladder, twirling,

a ridiculous girl, hungry for pie
and ceremony, devoted to bad
jokes, my bed a balloon, a whole city
rising in morning light, but at sunset
the desert gathers, drips into my mouth.
I can tell the future with my toothaches
but did not predict the long hours of waiting
on top of the roof for the wrong parade.

The hours are burnt toast, the coffee like rain,
and karma keeps flirting with the wrong girl—
someone soft, open, big hipped, wide angled,
her teeth cracked, her grittier song held back.

Seasoned

On this rooftop she sings like a siren
tonight, woman in a skirt of weather,
hem of infinite light. Strangers pass,
looking up to the source of song, but
can see only the frost of her ankles,
a swirl of snowflake in winter sky.

Underground her wail is molten, private
and forgotten. She has been transparent
but not anymore. Her see-through skin
now crimson, everything banging in
her bones. She will not be distracted from
dark pots dripping on the stove of rage.

Somewhere it is always cold, but she can't
police the temperature, though she tries,
grasps at night glitter like a baby,
new to this world. Sapphires drape her hips
but these shiny keys do not unlock
the spring leaf breeze place she revels in.

Far-off moon, her fingers cannot catch it.
She wants to hold its icy hand but time
keeps bending, evidence dripping into
the numb past. Her wardrobe about to blow.
One hot string connects her to my heart
where she sways to sleep's dark sonata.

My Mother Imagines the Weather as Music

Rain darkens gold brick and clay;
my mother hears melodies
swelling against the trapdoor.
Leaves tumbling to fragile
and familiar rhythms
of good and evil, long notes
like the glow of surrender.
It's evolution, wanting
to know morning in one's throat,
the composition of clouds
in the shape of regret. Her
body melts in the salsa
sun, a song that gleams from her
eyes. Possibilities sewn
in air, her arms grasp plates of
ache. A mother is a root,
a universe of cells; we
live in her cloudless sky, dance
in the color of her shade.

Evolution's Kitchen

Biologists demand a garland
of children, but I have neglected
any theory of origins.
My oven holds another cake,

fluid with cream, a complex miracle
of light and language, Miles Davis
on the radio, friends coming by.
Meaning-filled, the rich batter.

My eggs surrender—no babies;
I do not mind the empty house.
I choose the bowl of sky, abundant
songs of the night garden.

Stir fine rain into honey; pour
into a warm nest. Now sleep if you can.
Grate nutmeg outside the windows;
the birds will never leave.

Black Diamond

Snakes encircled my grandmother's hips
as she swayed to rhythms of a blue
guitar, heels striking sparks in the dark,
hypnotizing traffic in the night
world. Women, pinched lean by loneliness,
imagined her undignified, their
lips bright with cruelty, baseball game
on the old radio, hands dipping
into the snuff box, inhaling deep.

Fingers tapered red, she slapped away
their cold judgments. Queen of Tomorrow,
hers was a special destiny,
a trick of time; she believed in lust,
ice cream, accidents, momentary
grace, recoiled from the long hum of want.

Pandora

She dares me to bury the tired clock,
empty its lungs of dust and spill our
chaos into ocean, where sweet
daylight goes under but does not die.

She comes to see me on my small green
boat; swimming before me, opens her
eyes deep under water and finds gold
waiting to be dug up from the core.

She knows I will drink her venom, fresh
in a crystal flute. Absinthe pooling
on a tongue trafficked in blame, black
its exploding vocabulary.

Or will my restless mind take apart
her lovely mouth? Then colors of
evil will be rubbed out of this world,
only a breath of love left for earth.

Despite Enough

Nights, she polishes the mirror of forgetting.
Eyes won't focus on lightning that dismantles
the dark field, refuses the recognizable
songs of mercy. In her gaze, horizon dissolves
to orange candy, dusk bleeding into torch.

No sweetness in the lonely cafeteria,
only the mean magic of distant comfort
taken intravenously. She's tried to eat
the fruit of war, but it's stained her grin. She's seen
an epidemic of damage to her soft, sugar teeth.

She welcomes the cold fairies of ignorance,
their dirt and shine. She can shoplift a scrap of
power, but cannot guess the moment of onslaught.
In the garden of nothing, her veins nuzzle
drugs of erasing—cash for stash, a hard dose.

Roof of the World Torn Away

Wisdom Cookie

Have I fallen and spilled into
this killing future, roof of the world
torn away, body just an empty
house where wind walks over
rafters of bone? Creatures masquerading
as people, lumps of flesh with broken
mouths and no rhythm. We've made it

to the end of consequences, sit
on a wedge of destiny never
foretold. Starved for sugar we
cannot appreciate the sound
of trees. Honeybees are holy,
but we've forgotten their fate.
Out on this unintended highway,

you reveal the law of rage as
a spiritual teaching. I ignore
all clues, try to save nothing.
The debris of knowledge means little
now, kept as it is inside the smashed
surf shops; still a person will pretend
to drown when summer does not come full on.

Smashed Atoms

With ginger tongues
we keep asking for
something we think we deserve.
But you can't get pennies
out of a naked universe,
regrettable as that is.

The hungry man's home is
sidewalk. His pockets, rivers
of mud. Even when he dances,
he's given just 5 cents, so he
goes about everywhere on tiptoe.
Nights, he curls beside freeway.

Do I deserve that which comes
to me? The moon melting
in rain like a popsicle,
lost dog worries the stick?
Voices spitting from kitchen sink,
their scratchy harmonies?

When we ask for change,
press our lovely claims, do we
cry for the consequences?
A sky full of smashed atoms,
small umbrellas bending,
dirty with acid raindrops?

It's the babies that haunt me,
their morning sunshine money songs.
They giggle and threaten
shy leaves burning the sky.
Thousands of them in pink tutus,
so small, so unregarded.

Of Disappearing

When the elephant is gone
what will we know of its lustrous eyes?
With the lungs of our planet full of mud,
and the white ice dying,
will we prowl the graveyards of language
to ask the time? There's evidence of night
in the cement sky, in the velocity of turning spokes.

Sharks remember another time,
remember the green waves and the source
of darkness. Adrift now in a world without water,
they bump and crash through streets in flame,
too narrow for the crumpled vehicles bleeding
at the right of way. Even in the deepest jungle,
still the weak are prey.

Hummingbird rips the flickering leaves.
The woman: what can she preserve but hurt?
Her bracelet carved from tusks, her shining fan
a candelabra. The stone of her skin
smooth as a wound. Her rooms echo with reckoning.
Her questions answered in rhyme.
Her smile too rosy to be real.

Bowed

Once I survived in the forest
in a house of silver leaves, drank
from the brown river and washed my
skin of grudges. I covered its
nakedness in rags and light, dropped
the predatory habits of
victors. I played with foxes that
crept by, ears flattened, tails trembling
until they understood me as
animal. They cleaned the blue ash
of accountability from
my slight fur and wrapped me in wind.

I left when someone bombed the moon.
It hung low on the horizon
then, wizened and brown. Beneath, we
were all naked, shaking. Waiting
for the coming storm, for the flood,
waiting for deer to run to our
sides, but they had disappeared. So
much heat in summer's light, golden
and lethal, as we deserved. On
the corner, old man banging his
venom cup. Just our clocks remained
unscathed, flicking their cleaving hands.

Spilled Keys

Say we destroy the restless bed,
its seasick vistas of nervous
invention, our gestures that
crisscross the days in a long
meditation on time.

Say we've got separation
burned into our DNA,
the same as our ancestors,
those that caused the golden light
to wane, that gambled the stars.

Say the energy of our
of our little adventures
has spilled across the planet
China to Mexico
nothing without side effects.

We might not miss scorpions,
a dark source of sustenance,
when their time has passed, but some
day surely someone will want
the medicine of their sting.

We, fidgeting continents
this cloudy morning, wander
away from the dead bedroom,
as if this world were not mantra,
and each chanted phrase not love.

Poof!

She wanted to keep the white air in a jar
keep it separate from the catastrophe of chemicals
keep it for a tomorrow she would not remember

She remembered the frogs and the bees,
an anniversary of spring, the river at night like dark silk
she remembered reading the book of the river

What happened to the water, woman courting
slow water with her stormy flesh, the traffic of eyes,
what happened to the eyes: were they ruined by what she sees?

There'd been a time when she read the book of the body
when the body was not a lump of meat
when the body was not separated into moments and facts

Did she create the fire in the brain?
Did her brain create the big machine that hollowed the sun?
Is it her impatience that blisters the beautiful world?

She could make a little jam with her name
make a slow cup of sometimes to scald her tongue
cast it like a spell out onto the gears and gizmos

After Prairie

We'll make wildfire from the newspaper
and, as the culture burns, we'll hear
ghosts whispering the winter wind,
wars unraveling through dark grasses,
mantras of oil and gold crackling
to cold sky, spreading ash over
fierce water. So many shot through
with holy dreams, even buffalo
transformed into Star People; they
whistle in the scorched fields, awake
and accustomed to jeweled flame.

Once we stirred hope in a bloody
kettle, consumed its spiced perfume;
that was before drugs imagined
our quiet end. The clock bubbles
on the stove; blankets throw themselves
to floor. Everything blackening
but you and I ignore the hard
sounds, the cat dancing against fear.
Perhaps we spill fire from our eyes,
wonder the scent of peppermint
gently folded inside old wool.

Earthbound

1.
My hunger chews at the machine
of the world. It's either gasoline
or food, and the automobile
is so shiny. All the seasons
falling now. We cakewalk around
the fouled waters. Seeds buried in
some backyard will see the fires
before they see the weary sun.

2.
Who keeps the artifacts of that
distant time? Who owns the toucans or
carnival lights? If the blind dog
forgets them, do they disappear?
Pictures bleached to chemical sky;
they mock our reddened eyes, control
the story of a once green past;
they own the story of after.

3.
But I'm a flippant sinner, just
a whisper of calliope
for a soul. My sunburned shoulders
wrapped in breeze, a bird of fun and
frenzy, unable to listen
or belong, My private song begs
for transcendence, but the promise
of a lost world is to starve the stars.

I'm Re-thinking My Halo

No One Taught Me to Pray

I'm rethinking my halo.
It shines the color of lethargy.

My shadow stirs above me,
a white bird in a cage of sky.

I keep a river in my pocket;
red fish tumble at my feet.

Again and again, I run
to the distress party, holding my plate.

I hear the bell, but stay
unmoving, under the ice table.

I came to curl inside the world,
rise until the whistle blows.

But my bones are heavy now,
and the spirit is impossible to feed.

Redeemed

Jesus was carrying blind kittens down
to the radioactive ocean
to wash their wounds in the troubled waters.
They churned in silver, each wet and howling
until I plucked them out, hidden in my
green sweater, promised not to forget, served
up cream and tears. I noticed Jesus had
no shadow; his flesh evaporated
into another world; spine became a
river, arms a dim road under moonlight.
Who could follow into eternity?
Some think it mysterious, but I will
be left behind, eating my dusty words,
red lips shiny with honey, eyes on fire.

Three Mothers

Our Lady of Smoke. She appears,
dissolving in small particles.
The whole sky recognizes her,
songs falling to sacred ground, seeds
infusing rivers, bowl of earth.

Our Lady of Rain. We hear her
symmetry, her uncountable
forms. Field and trees and fruit long for
her ephemeral prayers. Oh,
her heart ceremonies fill us.

Our Lady of Stones, her womb our
house, this land no one remembers,
land of justice, of love. After
everything burns, hers is the form
of the world, its devastated fruit.

Bodhisattva

O
Lady,
climb back down
through smoky skies,
bullet-kissed mornings
and plutonium rains;
forgive us the fallen birds
rivers stippled green with metals
seeds choked under nothing but torched stars.

We who remain on the blasted earth
have lost our root, planted in bombed
dirt, blame seeped into the clouds.
Where now do we belong?
I can no longer
describe sunlight,
find water,
or know
home.

Yes,
Lady,
your eyes are
deep moons between
worlds; your arms provide
a house of the future.
Do not relinquish us. Carve
us into new form, let your knife
remember our essence, our first shape.

Let us reverberate like the leaves
of the first sapling, alone on
a mountain, stealing the last
warmth for our stiff limbs. Time
gives up its symbols
in sympathy
for you, Lady.

One sound, now
all is
still.

Non-being

Form brings the taste of summer,
covers spirit in cupcakes
flavored with orange daylight,
caresses the cheek with breeze.
It captures our eyes, then our
vision, tells us to serve,
to count and measure the waves.

The world swallows my footsteps,
plucks breath from the hole of my
mouth. Night takes my words; in their
place, butterflies migrate to
the water. Amber wings glow
in firelight, sound almost like
petals sighing in the trees.

Formless, I stop spinning, free
from the ego's paddle-wheel.
I sing with the helixes,
vibrate the sun's frequency.
Everything and nothing
not opposites, but pulsing
in a wider ocean.

Mostly

I wanted nothing more
nothing anymore

except when the freeway river
burned gold, that moment before night

That time I found, sometimes,
music in the light, staining my eyes

I hid from my sentient vision
I left a lot of things—

pots, pans, clock, knife
dog, cat, the never children

Whether I left or stayed
at the core I was learning to move

to change until the sun changed too
a gold spot on my retina

a plate of morning—
purples, yellows, greens

That it was pretty was a scrap of cruelty
I wanted everything

but I was mostly grateful
for my small bowl, blazing.

Wonder

The afterlife was a blur.
If there was beauty there, or trouble,
I didn't know. I was tempted
not to stop at all—so much speed
in the cereal bowl; a thousand miles
from jail to being stardust
inside the galaxy's polka dot
refrigerator. I felt I was trespassing
on this city of death. I tasted
its sour coffee, bounced on beds
of sky. It wasn't for me.
I had never prayed to the pointy hats.
On the other side of the door
were pickles and chocolate, money
and fire. I had to escape,
blackbirds my navigation device.
Maybe I would burn for it later,
but until that time,
I would not wonder, but sing.

TERRY WOLVERTON

Terry Wolverton is author of eleven books of fiction, poetry and creative nonfiction, including *Embers*, a novel in poems, and *Insurgent Muse: Life and Art at the Woman's Building*. In addition, she has edited fifteen successful compilations, including (with Robert Drake) the Lambda Literary Award-winning *His: brilliant new fiction by gay men* and *Hers: brilliant new fiction by lesbians*, volumes 1, 2, and 3. She has also collaborated with composer David Ornette Cherry to adapt *Embers* as a jazz opera.

Terry has received the Judy Grahn Award for nonfiction from the Publishing Triangle, a fellowship in poetry from the California Arts Council, and a COLA Fellowship from the City of Los Angeles Department of Cultural Affairs, among other acknowledgments.

Terry has taught creative writing in community settings for over three decades; in 1997, she founded Writers at Work, a creative writing studio in Los Angeles, where she teaches fiction, creative nonfiction and poetry. She is also an Associate Faculty Mentor for the MFA Writing Program at Antioch University Los Angeles. Additionally, she is a certified instructor of Kundalini Yoga.

From 1976-1989, she was an active participant at the Woman's Building, a public center for women's culture, creating art projects, teaching, serving on the Board of Directors and as the organization's Development Director and Executive Director. Since 1982, she has also provided management consulting services to nonprofit organizations, sole proprietor businesses and individual artists.

Website: http://terrywolverton.com.

www.ingramcontent.com/pod-product-compliance
Lightning Source LLC
Chambersburg PA
CBHW021158090426
42740CB00008B/1145